Augers

Books by Paula Rankin

By the Wreckmaster's Cottage (1977)
Augers (1981)

AUGERS

poems by

Paula Rankin

**Carnegie-Mellon University Press
Pittsburgh 1981**

Feffer and Simons, Inc., London

Acknowledgments

Acknowledgment is made to editors of the following magazines in which most of these poems first appeared:

Ark River Review: "Getting the Truth to Come Clear";
Ascent: "Two Lovers on Bridge in Winter"
Back Door: "Concerning a Dog Hit in Backwoods Tennessee"
Beloit Poetry Journal: "Foundry Poem"; "Two Poems for the Blood"
Carolina Quarterly: "Bedtime Story"
Chowder Review: "Losing Rings"; "Thinking of Others"
Georgia Review: "Shared Visions"
Kalliope: "The Clothesline Body"
Kansas Quarterly: "Love in Magnolia Cemetery"; "Provisions"; "Tenants: To Keep Us Carefully Moving"
The Nation: "At the Wharf, Yorktown: For all Tracks Made in Sand"
New Orleans Review: "Something Good on the Heels of Something Bad"; "The Woman Who Built Her House on the Sand"
Oconee Review: "The Recurring March Dream"
Ohio Review: "Callers"
Old Hickory Review: "Weathering"
Outerbridge: "Hansel Revisited"; "Miracles"
Plainsong: "Senility"
Ploughshares: "In the Calendar Square of the Dream"; "Poem for Exchange of Habitat"
Poem: "For Workers in Wood and Dirt"; "For Vacationers at Endless Caverns Campground"
Poetry Northwest: "The Man Who Invented Fireworks"
Poetry Now: "Working Third Shift
Quarterly West: "For My Mother, Feeling Useless"; "Tending"; "For the Child Drowned in the Well of Black Water"
raccoon: "Hot Bath in an Old Hotel"
Tar River Poetry: "Teleportation"
Three Rivers Poetry Journal: "Poem for the Tick"; "Wrestling with the Angels of Intention"

The publication of this book is supported by grants from the National Endowment for the Arts in Washington, D.C., a Federal agency, and from the Pennsylvania Council on the Arts.

Library of Congress Catalog Card Number 80-70565
ISBN 0-915604-45-0
ISBN 0-915604-46-9 pbk.
Printed and bound in the United States of America
First Edition

Contents

For Terry, Jenny, & Walter

In the Calendar Square of the Dream

The whole square turns to ice:
It is a cube popped free
from the past's causation,
from future's effect, so that my father,
long dead, is back at the wheel
of our '49 Chevy, steering my mother,
my sister, and me on treadless tires
over the ice;
though even in the dream
we know he is dead,
we trust ourselves to his traction,

even when he jumps out
and we notice the others
jumping out, leaving hundreds of cars
free-wheeling, even when we see him
and his friends directing traffic,
pointing to chuckholes and patches
of ice, even when we see him flagging
wreckers, we are so happy to see him
back in control.

Teleportation

Thus, in every case of a strange appearance, one should look for another of a strange disappearance.—**Phenomena: A Book of Wonders.**

I do not speak of those
Who inexplicably vanish
forever, but of those taken away
and brought back, stuttering
outlandish alibis. I think of their falling
like red rain on the farmer,
shearing his tobacco, veining the dumb vision
of cows. Or of their landing
in plaid flannel shirts
like neighbors. But what of the ones
who step forth from the woods
leaving fur in their tracks?

Mostly I think of their being dropped,
wandering and bewildered, calling out
the names of old friends.

They remind me of lovers
who wake every day to a strange place
and try to give it a name:
home,
room left behind
by men and women who spent years
breaking it in. And drove one night
to the grocery store
for a pack of cigarettes.
Or so they intended.

Getting the Truth To Come Clear

"His truth is clearest when it is poised against a system of lies."
— **Mark Jarman in _University Publishing_**

I asked a ninety-three-year-old woman,
Of everything that has happened,
what do you remember most?
She said, Once, as a child, I hid
under the porch while they rode off
on horses to find me. They got the whole county
out riding but they never came close.
When my parents grew sorry enough
I crawled out
and they went and got my cat back
from the neighbors.
Is this one measure of Truth,
I ask, the moment that leaps
across all others,
furred with consequence?

All my life I've been a sucker
for Love, Peace, as well as the darker abstractions,
have gone off after the least shreds of evidence
rumored stashed inside faces like cupboards,
awaiting my hunger. Now it is Truth
I hear will come clear
if only I choose the right backdrop.

What is the process for collecting
reliable lies? No pale equivocations:
I need the honest-to-God lies-in-the-teeth,
the indisputable deceptions, such as
"I answered your letter last week";
"My teeth are my own"; "Last night
I saw no one." I need to cover one wall
with black flannel lies
sponging light. I'll tack our photographs
there to whisper how we'll go on
forever. Then one by one
I'll move our real faces across the wall
to see what refuses absorption.
what comes clear as bone against topsoil,
for it may not be skull after all:
it may, please God, be the eyes,
or soft coils of brain;
it may be the tongue's gift
for cursing, benediction.

Bedtime Story

If the Devil don't want nothing
he must want something.

If he ain't barely imaginable
he must be red fluorescent skin,
spikes jutting from forehead,
a shredded grin, as in *gnashing of teeth*.

If he seen you
it's too late.

But hide, hide under the covers,
may be he gets confused
in his tenses
and agreements. May be
he thinks you signed something
when you ain't signed nothing at all.

Tell him you can't hardly write.

Miracles

Because I want to believe,
I stare at the procession
of those who come to be healed:
they lay afflictions at his feet
like addresses obscene callers dial from
when we, the as-yet-unafflicted,
bed down for the night.

Everything is here that is needed:
river for total immersion, oil
for annointing, copperheads for the faithful

and the demons whose number is legion,
who have been through this before;
they quake in their human apartments,
steeling themselves for the shock
of raw air and the hunt of old wounds
for new flesh to lie down in.

Hansel, Revisited

Why us? It is a question I often ask,
back safe in my father the woodcutter's
cottage, my stomach full, my stepmother
snoring as she never did
those nights when we were poor.

Then I asked for bread
and received it, when what I needed
were stones. You know by now
our wanderings, retrievals, our feasting
on shingles of cake the crone bakes
in her own oven, likely as a stepmother's
melting heart. But what I remember

is the cage and my grip on chicken bone;
more than waking in the heart
of a forest with nothing to track
I remember thrusting the proof of bone
to a myopic woman.

Sealed in the happily ever after,
we are still called forth
from time to time for reasons
I'm not sure of, though metaphor-for-life
is often cited. Yet when I read us
like a story we didn't know we were in,
I see how narrow escape is,
how it depends on witches blind
and slightly retarded, on mastering the aim
of one's bones until they give the lie
to anything hungry.

Poem for Miners

Does everyone wake up one day
to find his vocation is looping
Texas interstate, odd country where,
no matter what pre-Neanderthal cell
his family began in, there is a counterpart,
—ocean, forest, rock, tumbleweed,
boom towns still on the map
of everyone's desert,

as if, with luck, a man might accidentally
veer down a ramp and stake a claim
on a family plot passed down to him
in a will burned before America?

Does everyone sooner or later wake
as I do now, inside so many other bodies,
sifting genes like a prospector panning for gold?

All I have of my Texas father
is a snapshot staring through credit cards,
through the cracked seam in my wallet
towards anything I pretend
is the object of his attention.
Father, I am low on luck, so forgive me
if I walk you up and down the tracks
of the Santa Fe, as if it will help you
lose weight, improve your circulation,
stoke coals into the failed furnace
of your heart. Is there anything here

I can hammer like a spike into railroad ties,
something so true I can finish
the unfinishable novel
about men who walk off
and keep walking
and never look back
except through eyes flattened
to fit inside wallets?

If I say I stand in Sweetwater, Texas,
asking this, I mean it as any town
where no Alamo overshadows other defeats—
one man going down at a time,
one descendant mining for the least
geiger count transmitted
in the unreasoning hope
he will know how to pass it down.

The Woman Who Built Her House on the Sand

I want to be here by the ocean
where nothing comes that I must learn
to love. How can anything with lessons
be love? I once knew a man
who called himself wise: he drew pictures
with fish spines on the damp sand,
saying, *heed, turn, flee.* I pressed
the whelk to my eardrum with its rush
of promises: wash away, wash away,
we will all wash away.

I have a new lover. Inside the cottage,
he oils his body for sun.
The one before made wine from dates
and pomegranates. How we loved, our skins whorling
like the insides of certain mollusks
I've collected, each time, after storm.

The ocean changes its colors, lapis, feldspar,
bdellium, manganese, and the onyx
that warns me each time to batten down.
But it is the sand that keeps me here,
because after many lives
I still cannot unriddle it as image,
composition, or simile: how is sand
like Abraham's descendants, Job's heaviness,
Solomon's largeness of mind? How is it ground
and poured into ovals I hold in my hand
and stare into?

Each time the sky blackens, the Lord's darts
needle the stilts of my cottage
toward the base of the dune.
Each time storm brews it dumps me to my knees:
I am going to die! I should have lived inland!

But each time it is the house
with my lover in it,
so instantly collapsible, scoured
from vision, as if I were the heart of sand's
riddling: how am I like what remains?

Appeased, the ocean glasses over,
deadly in its terrible beauty.
I rake the beach, pocketing shards of angel wings
and abalone for my collection,
the tray I keep as proof that happiness was here,
like love, that silt is nothing
faced with memory's hold on what matters.

I will order fresh lumber.
I will take a new lover.
I will listen to the words in the whelk,
but I will not heed them.
For what if I had nothing to lose?
What if Loss had nothing in it
but the Lord's giving and taking away,
what if I slept untroubled by portents and dreams?

Even now, the sands shift under me,
open to the least brush of wind.
Last night I dreamed a sailor's turning
his back on the sea
after seeing me, in his dream,
waving and waving and waving.

Tenants: To Keep Us Carefully Moving

In books we have read how counterparts
move with us
through apartments
on the other side of oceans
or some life before this one.

How often I have tried to shake hands
with just one of the people inside me,
the child rummaging through daguerrotypes
in the attic, trying each eye on for size,

the woman I have not yet become
who rocks in and out of her shapes,
knitting the most stretchable of sweaters.

Always they refuse my attempt at casual
contact. They stare out for hours
as if rooms-to-let signs were hung
all over my body, patiently waiting the foot
on the stairwell. Nights I sense ears pressed

to corridors inside all of us
as we pick our ways home, slide faster
than we ever dreamed
down bannisters, trying hard to recall
all we were taught about speaking to strangers.

Provisions: For a Book of Poems Received on New Year's Eve

for David

It is the last day of the year.
Beyond your book, taupe buntings peck
through leaves brittle as hands that finally let go
when there's nothing left to cling to.
Birdwatchers say they are omens
of snow, cracking seeds like dreams
everyone has of storing enough
to thwart the hard freeze. If I say
I crack your words like this,
holding them in my lap, your 3×5 glossy face
staring out the back cover
through my jeans, through floorboards
towards the core of this planet,

you will understand I breathe in terms
of distance covered, remembering the migrations
of artic terns from ice to Africa,
of all wings homing without compass.
What is survival but forgetting
the ones that fly into lighthouses,
the hurricane-shredded, the mast-filleted?

I remember the gull was our bird, the way
it met any scraps tossed and transformed them
into extra wingbeats, the only kind of power
worth our coveting. I remember this and more
as I go out before snow with your book
and a bowl of crumbs, facing Arctics head-on
like a woman in a backwoods Georgia church
who tests her faith by outstaring one rattler
a day. I scatter breadcrumbs like surplus
Eucharist wafers while your photograph watches,
daring the cold to set up anything
but temporary quarters.

For the Child Drowned in the Well of Black Water

Once I defined drowned childhood
by child starlets I saw on TV,
fame come upon them so early
that they believed all the fan mail,
pouted when on-the-set-private tutors
pushed multiplication tables,
pitched fits if off-stage mothers
fixed tuna fish for lunch.

The day your mother brought you to me
she marked an X where her name should have filled
the blank granting permission for field trips;
Welcome, Teresa, come in, I said, offering a hug
you backed off from so fast
I saw the outstretched arm
must speak differently to each of us.

You spoke to no one for months.
How many days I hid you in the bathroom
pinching nits from your hair, bathing you
in warm sink water, pinning a ribbon
in your strawed hair, erasing what I could
of your smell of acrid, dried urine. You never spoke
but grinned, baring all your rotten teeth, knowing
that for one day, no one would shove his chair
away from you, no chants of "she stinks"
would machete the wax in your eardrum.

When you finally talked
I found myself praying you wouldn't,
that I would miss some minimal bliss
of ignorance. You talked about fathers,
how yours walked in brand new every week, sometimes
two or three times in one day,
and that once a father who stayed a whole month
actually learned your name
and brought you a book of paper dolls
you still slept with, having never snipped
them from their backgrounds of slick whiteness.

My one hope was that you were a pathological
liar. But you weren't, and then how I needed
to teach you of other rooms
some people grow up to live in,
where supper is often tuna or a cheap grade
of ground beef, but doors are left open
for entries, exits, some approximation of love.

When all the other children were way beyond names,
could mimic Dog, Cat, Snake, any shape of holiday,
all you gave me were sheets filled with T's aimed
in all directions. All this high purpose of mine
failed so long ago that some nights I can barely
remember your face. I try not to ask
if you have a new collection of fathers
all of whom know you by name
for one night, and leave ten dollars
on the table for the privilege.
If so, I hate them most of all
because they use a name
you never wrote on a page where T's collided,

a page I still hold
in shaking hands as if fingers could braille
the secret of how you have come to be
whoever you are,
as if I could go to your mirror and stare
until glass melts into a well
of black water, where objects take turns
floating up to the surface—dolls, jump ropes,
skates, a grosgrain ribbon, a snag-toothed grin,

then plummet for their third and final drowning.

The Lady Loved a Sailor

Each time I'm pushed to choose
between a last stand
against the odds against us
and a last lying down
in despair, you swagger down the brow
of the destroyer harbored in my memory,
its anchors plunged deep as blind fish.

I call you forth
to shake in the face of Fate
one of its failures. If it can be tricked
by two tiny hucksters
burying their secrets like bulbs
planted by the drifter
for the plain, unmarried schoolteacher,
then it can spring a leak
soon as an innertube hissing air,
a sky snowing manna,
a life draining out of a body.

There was no walking on water,
but there were moments we rode like surfers
on ocean breaking under us
with its heave of undertow and silt.

And still the magic
happens: my neighbor's sow
nurses kittens he's given her
to eat; purposes are thwarted
even here, in Tennessee,
where I came to grow mature
and acquiescent, to put aside the child's fascination
with dark mirrors, that faith which swears
she saw hands silvering themselves
across her dimly lit face.

For Vacationers at Endless Caverns Campground

A grizzly stares from a plaque,
his jaws frozen into the shape
of what may have been his last growl,
but then even the most skillful taxidermy
has limits: it does not know
how to work with real blood
or stuff eyes with peripheral vision

any more than I can call up
real campers to defy the "Abandoned" sign
nailed across the entry for bodies
once bent on getting away from it all.

Yet there is still an air of taking time
off: stones circle kindling that seems to wait
only for least wind and anyone's match
to begin again the old story
of why some burn
while others spit at what flames
try to tell them they're made for.

Unable to stake a tent in undergrowth
like a promise which someone homeless
could still enter, lie down in,
ward off one night's frost with,
I camp inside a 1930 photograph of here
when stones kept fire in its place
and a fountain pumped from caverns,
held a sign guaranteeing "Safe Water."
I think of bodies wheeled or limping here
for healing, wanting miracles to defy
my cynic's belief that there is
such a thing as safe water,

but it tastes funny,
rare as the time
I decided against adultery.

Nonetheless I continue to rummage
through evidence, a mold-skinned book
where lodgers' names still flow
from tips of fountain pens, the ink
never skipping as mine does
as I press down hard to sign in,
determined to be included in the least flourish,
scroll, loop of calligraphy
that left home to come here
for healing, went back to fill out
new kinds of checks, shopping lists, the letter
everyone wishes he'd written or received

For Workers in Wood and Dirt

I remember one who did not go to pieces
when the children left through the hole
in everyone's house: hammering
was what he did best, and making knots
in lumber work for us
like a promise passed down in wills
bequesting bookshelves, cupboards, walls.

I'd stumble through his house,
breaking two toes once on a doorstop
that was nowhere near a door,
cursing that a man would cram
liveable space with two-by-fours,
nail kegs, sawhorse, a broadloom
of splinters, as if, at the touch
of a serious hand, wood urged new taproots
that might plunge, and retrieve,
the lost bones of children.

It was she who had nothing to do with her hands
except dustpan a life's shavings.
The day he broke his wrist
I found them sitting on a half-finished
bench, asking the questions everyone asks
when the wrong bone breaks
when the wrong house goes up in smoke
when the good die young.

All I had to offer
was what I'd brought, an assortment of bulbs
fresh from the dark in my cellar,
their papery skins hardly a believable promise
of what I wanted them to believe in:

tiger lilies punching their necks into air,
blinding those who drive past
to get groceries, go to work, carpool children,
until they have no choice but to stop
and ask the owners if all they used
was dirt and bare hands.

Foundry Poem: For All Children Burned Alive

It is Friday, the day for fish
and mold-pouring: I can still see the men
peeling waxed paper from trout, unrolling
tin from sardines, waiting for ovens
to finish their work
so that something might come
of melted iron: wheels, anvils,
spikes for keeping trains
forever on their tracks.

My grandfather once turned his smoked face
to me and explained smelting, how all boiled down
to ore and slag, how sand learned
not to shift when pressed far from wind into casts.
He did not say how he used the same process
for raising his children, their skins on fire
not for his Lord but from their own core.
The furnace was no metaphor, but the backslider's real
foundry, its latch loose enough for a child to open,
loose enough to open on its own
the way it opens on me
again and again without warning.

I stand in my grandfather's abandoned ironworks,
pretending I can question his hard, fixed visions
of evil and good, his dark saints coagulating
in molds men crush their bones on.
I stand here unable to swallow
slag eating the roof off my mouth,
fearing I might prove the body's flexibility,
its knack for being melted and reshaped
into ash, bone chips, cables of my brain

where despite all I can do
I feel arteries hardening
like iron coming into its own.

Working Third Shift

I have a friend
who volunteered
to get away
from people.
He is part of the road crew
that scrapes dogs
off the highway;
sometimes raccoons, skunks.
Once a cow took them all night.
Mornings when the road looks wet
they've hosed it. He said
I'd never guess what a road
would be like
if not for them.

They like to work alone.

The Man Who Invented Fireworks

Once a man with Roman candles gunpowdering
his head went out at night
to find sky's inattention
resembling too much the ceiling
towards which an invalid strains
his dimmed eyes. Or perhaps

he simply weighed the various acts
by which one is remembered
and chose combustion, the vocation
in which whole moments are strung
on short fuses, tattooing air with vermilion,
emerald, flumes of white fire.

He may have foreseen us,
huddled by one shore of Jekyll Island,
awaiting promised flags, chrysanthemums, riders
pinwheeling unbuckable stallions;
and if so, predicted a market
for charcoal, saltpeter flaring from mouths
of medieval statues, while priests
uttered prayers on atonement.

He may have sensed that the path to attention
would not change much,
that those with strained eyes
would still be around
drop-mouthed at the trick of ignition,
of getting shows not only off the ground
but shot through the sky's epidermis
and the skins of each other's eyes,
a searing of tissue
to last the whole length
of its moment.
For who gets enough attention?

Perhaps he knew how some nights
these collisions of stars, shells, saxons
would still be the only holes
worth congregating for,

how that is all we would own,
that, and the shared, humbling aftermath
of backdrop.

For My Mother, Feeling Useless

Some people grow chalky dust on their skin
like leaves on a dirt road.
My mother, who would not run to the drugstore
without clean underwear, stockings,
hair pinned, two spots of blusher,
who believed everything mattered,
now sighs, *no need, no need.*

Who am I? she asks
of my father's, my sister's, and my faces
on the wall, under glass.
Her face lies on them
until it cannot bear the likenesses.

If she goes out for supper
no one knows if she comes back
or keeps driving
into the ocean
or down a dirt road spraying dust.

On her last plane ride
she had a vision
of being taken up
beyond the top cloud;
then she heard a voice
telling her she had to go
down, she was needed.

When I was a child,
she owned two dresses,
many aprons. There was great need
for her hands in the sink,
in the threadbox with needles.

There was great need
when my grandfather's brain
turned to mush, when my father lost
his sense of touch.

I leave my house
and go down the clay road
where the trees smother
into ghosts of themselves.
A car spins past, coating my legs
with gravelly powder
and I warn, *Back off, dark space,*
I've got connections.
My husband and children saw me leaving.

Poem for the Tick

We never hear him drop
from a leaf or pine needle
onto one pore. While we're camping out
he's camping in where our skin closes
like tent flaps.

Hard-shelled, he bloats like any poacher
with no heart for his own blood
while ours pumps like a lover
loving only himself. We want
to pick him off before he bloats
with connections to the brain.
Even after checks of our scalps
we're sure he's still attached,

the heavy hidden drinker in all of us,
the real reason our hairs turn gray
and the skull sets up camp
behind our faces.

Something Good on the Heels of Something Bad

When things get too bad, as they usually do,
I try to remember the friend who told me
"Troubles are money in the bank."
She should have known,
and if I go outside
it is not to run from a pack of dogs,
breaking my leg on the ice;
it is not to crunch through the snow
to Broad Street and talk again to the man
who wheels himself into the bar
at the end of each day; it is not to hear him
say, "tomorrow's take will be better";
it is not to watch the bartender extend his credit.

I do not go out
to run into the ghost of my grandmother,
wringing her pale hands, asking
why I am all that is left
of her green chromosomes, complaining
of insufficient compensation.

There are authentic accounts
of reversals: last week I met a man
who'd lost his job, his wife, his children
and just when he'd given up hope,
he won the lottery,
his father left him a farm in Minnesota,
and a woman he liked even better showed up.

Look out, my friend said,
if nothing's missing,
if everyone you love has all his parts.
Look out if sky floats full of cumulus.
And sometimes, she said, when things are bad
they have to get worse, much worse,
before sorrow is torn into scraps of redeemable paper.

I am going out in this blizzard
to track the bright sides of drifts,
of wheels spun loose into ditches
I am going out to listen for the beast
that comes sniffing at the heels of bad news.
I have to believe he's out there, that
he's already picked up the scent
of crushed will, heartsblood, that any moment
I will hear him eating the awful evidence.

Wrestling With the Angels of Intention

It is a troublesome dream,
patched together
to repair my own guilt.

If it is true that dreams stitch
what they are given—
shreds, scraps of consciousness,
faces seen in checkout lines

then there must be more than one self
making sense of it,
more than one angel
debating, rowing up and down streams

of the body, collecting allegiances
that float there, the faces
of love we never let go of
even in sleep. Oh, the judgments pronounced

by nearsighted, farsighted,
arthritic, loose-jointed, sane and mad
angels, the endless debates tottering
brinks between heaven and hell:

I wake troubled,
for who truly wants to be evil?
I wake with renunciation on my lips,
determined to balance the feet
on floors planked with good intentions

while outside, the wind is unwrapping news
like horoscopes I should have read
but didn't; it is in such a hurry
to hand me the wings that have won.

Weathering

January: the dark comes down,
the air brittle with predictions.
I will not be going out:leg in a cast,
I am trying to keep
to safe, small places

trying not to think
of the cow walking dumbly up the embankment onto the highway
or the child found under the bridge
or the nursing home in east Nashville
where the wiring is faulty.

I am trying not to think
of the dumb, the small, or the helpless.

I am trying to be very quiet.
Perhaps I will go
 unnoticed.

Then I hear my small son
singing to the darkness
as he slides down the driveway
home.

Tending

It's no secret I've failed
with all our gardens. There were the tiger-lily bulbs
I never split that died of strangulation,
the roses with skeleton leaves,
the chrysanthemums with fungus,
and always the centipede grass with its root system
of runners.

So much you think you yank up
goes on with its underground tunnels
siphoning water and sun,
feeling for another nudgable crumb of dirt.

My children, I need to tend you more carefully
than gardens. When we moved here, deadnettle and thistle
had already taken over and it was almost a relief
to throw up my hands, say,
"All is lost," and turn inward.
And some things have happened to me
that have made me feel we have no more chance
than stems left to choke and rot,
that the only roots will be those tunnels
sucking us into the earth.

But I will never tell you.
Because maybe the yard is outside,
not connected to us, maybe weeds take over
everything but us. Maybe,
just because I fail in weeding out
my own duplicities, leaving them to run riot
all over my body, it doesn't mean
I can't learn some saving pull for you,
my arms towing you in over deep water.

The possibility alone keeps me reaching.

Losing Rings

You blame me for losing my rings,
three in five years.
I say, "My fingers lose weight with loving."
I too have wondered at the ease
with which they slid off undetected:
one into dirt my hands dug out for bulbs,
another into river,
and one I last saw pulling sleeves
from a laundromat dryer.

None had enough scratches to be a symbol
for unending love, so when I think about them,
I do not think of gold circumferences
but of the space inside and what fills it:
somewhere dirt, muck on river bottom,
lint in a stranger's pocket
are the finger I should have grown,
the one I keep trying to fatten
or if nothing else works, coat with glue.

Finally you turn to me, empty-handed,
saying, Here is the ring of imagination,
imagine love that goes on forever,
imagine this is the last ring you will be given,
imagine anything you need to make it fit.

My fingers are nearly all bone.
But I imagine a ring shrinking like skin.

Thinking of Others

My mother's solution
for my father's depression:
Think of others worse off than you.
And for each step he took with his walker
she found a man with no legs,
no wheelchair, no woman to pull him back
from the brink.

For each hold he couldn't keep on a saucer
she knew a man with hands blown off
in a factory explosion.

When the numbness spread to his tongue,
she reminded him of the camp
where prisoners' tongues were lit or cut out.

For each face he could no longer make out,
there were babies born blind,
dumped in trashcans.
There was Helen Keller.
There was the man with two heads
growing right out of his spine.

She knew people with none of their parts
who kept going.
For each feeling my father lost
she offered him Pain
and what it could feel like
if he could feel.

Poem for Exchange of Habitat

There is always something outside
that wants in: again tonight,
I cannot back the car out of the garage
for the animals that gather. I think
of moving back to the city,
where not once did I choke
on the spray of wild skunk
on my path to the dryer, not once
did I intercept the nocturnal missions
of cats, possums, dogs. What is this pull

towards the hum of my machines, toward
tables, sleeves, flesh, lamplight,
flicked-down dark? When they move up close,
the home that bounced off their eyes
is one I cannot give them,
though my own stares twisting these hills
prove my willingness to trade
our Lists-of-What-Is-Denied.

Why else would I sit up so late
writing letters to the dead
or vanished? I seal them and carry them out
to their box by the roadside, hoist
the red flag and wait. I know
they are out there, re-estimating
the contents, sizing the exchange.

Relocation: From Water to Hills

I used to believe we would turn into ocean
salt bite by salt bite, each diminution
unnoticed, yet granular as sand.

Now I think we will turn into hills,
their curves bending and shaping
our bodies, their grasses staining our skin.

I thought Tennessee was the south
but my son came home with frostbite
purpling his calf. Last winter,
bound together
in this house for two months,
we ate, slept, made love
without heat, without power.
We tried to find a new way of needing
each other. Would anyone find us
come spring? And the people we left:
don't they turn into something other?
How will we recognize our mothers?

Yet to say we are homesick
is to tell a fable with animals in it
whose motives and morals stay simple enough
for a child. We came here, after all,
because love in that place was too easy.

The Clothesline Body

Each night I leave my dress on the line
between the Sumacs.
I unbutton the bodice and cuffs
so the dark can fall in easily,
taking my body's place
without the limits my hands
put on reach, my feet put on movement,
my head puts on knowing and loving.

This body's mouth fills with fireflies
and leaves, a broth of lichen,
mothwings. This body's hair is so long
it wafts the hills. Part of it lies
in the creek, filling with mayflies
and algae. A crayfish cracks out of its shell
and hides under a rock in my eardrum.
My tongue turns into wind.

Mornings, I go out and put on the dress,
buttoning it clear to the neck and wrists,

and wake the children with the touch
that barely knows where it's been.

The Recurring March Dream

Bored with being snowbound, the wind
picked up anything it found and threw it:
a garbage can's lid landed on our windshield,
splattered as a giant's dinner plate

with something green, dried, fibrous.
Everywhere the air was spiked with sharp edges—
gravel, branches—all headed for us,
while mateless shoes that had lain in ditches

for months shuffled again with that awful hope
I had seen lifting shoes at the Home
for Abandoned Children. I wanted to stop
and try them on to see if this was the time

I would replace someone else's body,
but we were running too late to give ourselves over
to wind. That night I dreamed again the bloody
trail that is always missing between air

and ground's collections of shoes, shirts, dwellings.
I dreamed again that some things, like love,
were too heavy to lift, that wind would save
its rescatterings and erasures for things

that left empirical holes when uprooted
or thrown down, that it would not waste
itself on us, for whom no needle, thread, paste
is needed when we open the air and step out.

Two Poems for the Blood

All night the corpuscles hum to each other
      Remember, as a child, the circle
of bones, vital organs, primeval caves
      you sat in with a needle poised
chanting rhythmically the rites of passage
      for pricking blood from the finger,
from body to body, each cell an aria
      feeding the need for closest kin —
attempting harmony, low notes flushed with descant.
      Where are they now, those other faces
All night the corpuscles hum to each other
      serious with allegiances sworn till doomsday,
of bones, vital organs, primeval caves,
      gone off to trace their own pulse:
chanting rhythmically the rites of passage
      does a molecule of yours still travel with them
from body to body, each cell an aria
      passing down to their children, a minute's mingling
attempting harmony, low notes flushed with descant —
      of blood taking hold like a spot on the lung,
All night the corpuscles hum to each other
      showing up only in an X-ray of memory,
of bones, vital organs, primeval caves
      vials on hospital shelves,
chanting rhythmically the rites of passage
      eyes burning from dark sockets with recognition
from body to body, each cell an aria
attempting harmony, low notes flushed with descant.

Love in Magnolia Cemetery

No one knows us here.
I could be Lelia Harlett, b. 1896,
my crinoline rustling through grass
on an errand of grief. Or we can be
the initials carved into the crepe myrtle bark
where Robert goes on loving Janice
despite sapsuckers, borers into heartwood,
the changing directions of wind.

Everything here
except granite
seems made for love, I say,
as you bite my shoulder
and Easter explodes with resurrections
of azalea, forsythia, dogwood.
There is even a pond
for lovers to comb water across their faces
like tears. And the wind here
never ceases its shuffling of leaves,
redispersing stories
from the four corners of earth,
the only denouement worth keeping track of.

Should we—here? In your eyes
I see the headlights of cars
driving home to soft beds.
If I were Lelia Harlett, my time
would have been up three years ago.

Love, I forgot to mention
someone we know is buried here.
I always save my best lies
for love. Look: magnolia buds knot
and swell towards July
and the space on our stones
still glares with uncut granite,
open-ended, waiting for legends.

Hot Bath In an Old Hotel

Asleep, you turn
on the knots in your neck
though I spent an hour
ironing your back with my knuckles.
We stiffen with travel.
I take off my clothes
and sit on the cold porcelain bottom
of the tub. I want it like this,
my spine slabbed and chilled
as a column of ice cubes.
Look, I can take it, I hiss
through my teeth, through the door.

I turn the handle
and lie back as water
scalds its way up like memories.
With each inch I lose a sadness.
By the time it reaches my neck,
I have forgotten who we are.

Callers

I accidentally dial
my own number.
The line is busy.
I wonder to whom
my friend talks
at this hour.
Then the digits
jungle like coins from slots
in my brain, and I know
I am calling myself.
I do not hang up
for five minutes.

Last week, I made
a similar mistake,
dialing my empty house
from a pay phone.
It rang one time
before I slammed the receiver
in panic,
certain that at any moment
the I
I left home
would answer, saying,
have a good time,
don't hurry back,
everything's waxed,
supper's simmering
without you.

For months
we have answered the phone
to heavy breathing.
The children are afraid;
my husband wants
an unlisted number.
Only I
feel relief
in pressing my ear
to someone else's
respiratory system.
Relief that I am not
the dialer,
that there is more
to this business
of contact
than overhearing the self
through busy signals,
more than leaving
oneself inside walls
only to panic
that she is the one
who inherits.

The caller
chose our number
out of millions.

Against such odds
I hang on
until he hangs up.

Fifty calls, and still
our breaths' timing is wonderfully
off. Our exhalations intersect
spasmodically.
We are not two
of a kind.

Shared Visions

"Our interest is in visions which are perceived by more than one person, and we are content to leave the explanations to others."
                                    —Phenomena: A Book of Wonders

Often more than one sees:
the rope standing on its end,
the boy shimmying up it
becoming a cloud; the ship
that lands in Kansas,
glowing all night in a field.

Those who see cannot help
but marry each other.

Years go by.
He still thinks of the night
a blue fog with hands and feet
walked on the water.
She remembers it as a lantern
swinging in the grip
of a drowned sailor.
Some nights it's the ascensions
of wings through the roof.
Some nights it's that woman in black
you could put your hand through
and promise never to forget.

Senility

I have never been
so many people at once
since my great-aunt Alice died.
Combing her patches
of hair, one minute I was the sister
in the lawn dress she'd wanted
for herself. She'd wave to me
through the drapes' leakage
of light. Veined with that light,
I turned into her husband,
come home from the field,
wanting supper, She'd tell me
to wait for the children.
Waiting, I became the child
who had vanished: "Why do you never come
to visit?" Once I was only the initial
carved into maple
in one of her Springs.

One minute I was her best friend.
The next I could be wind
from the north. I was cold,
and by then, I began looking for myself
in earnest. I had to be in her,
lodged between the blanks.

Two Lovers on Bridge in Winter

It is not clear what they love,
as they lean over the rail
in opposite directions

staring across the blue ice.
Where snow sleeves the pilings,
there are tiny tracks pricked

like maps for ascent, but there are no
birds in the picture. The sky
is immense, and has the pallor of skin

in nursing homes. In the foreground,
frozen branches scratch the air;
pine boughs look as though, any moment,

they will give up their luggage of snow
and crash through bridge, lovers, lake.
The lovers' stares make fissures

and hairline cracks in the dream
of walking on water. They are so tiny,
set against all that will happen!

I move in close and ink third arms
for both of them, placing them
hand over hand to clutch the same span

of railing before the wind
picks up, and snow buffs its slow erasures.
I swivel their profiles and have them embrace

for all whose dreams crack
like ice thawing. See how carelessly

they breathe
or hold their breath.

The Last Dream

Say in the last dream
we really do float
out of our body, staring back
stunned by what seems to have been,
all along, two of us.

We tap the doctor
on the shoulder,
but he is occupied.
Is this the face
we meant to leave on a pillow,
the suit we'd have chosen
from so many? And what are those words
our mother keeps repeating
because they were our last?

Hear me, each loved one says
to our other ears
and we do, funneling
our new molecular structure
into one magnanimous gesture

that fails. Next thing we know
we are loose
on the roof, waiting for our name
to be called
from the Roll-of-All-Possible-Winds.

Concerning A Dog Hit In Backwoods Tennessee

Only a moment ago, you were thinking
how, despite the everywhere hills,
their peaks and pits seemed negotiable,
as if someone had taken the time
to pour them from a slow truck,
working with the tumbling rhythm
of the part of Earth that decided, Here all
will be headed up or down, and always know which,
leaving guess and surmise
to riders of flat stretches through desert, coastline.

The scenery, you'd have said,
was picturesque, a background for a painting
which kept to its place, allowing you
your God-given space as focal point
in foreground; at most, one or two
twister-whipped pines, rocks, blades of rye grass
may have leaned toward you
as if wanting more deeply into the blur
of your attention. Only afterwards
do you remember this and try to guess
what might have happened had you stopped
to hear their versions of what wind had done
to them, along with downpours, droughts, late freezes.
Look at us: we are not as we were
and somehow we want you to notice our becoming
something else, for whether blessing or curse,
this is the way we keep happening.

But that would have taken more than you could spare
of a shortening life. Then: Dog. Fur the color
of the parched field-weeds it burst from
to leap at your car, and you not knowing
who it was
that slammed your brakes, skidded into ditch
after the dull thump
of dog suddenly lying in your rearview mirror's
inadequate patch of hindsight.

Struck dumb as stone-brain, you sense only
that something must be done: what is one's duty
here? Grim tales of those who spin getaways
in rubber. *Help,* you say to anything
that might listen. Climbing out, with only one foot
on pavement, you watch in disbelief
dead dog rising, shaking tire-trakcs from fur,
loping across field as if transfused
with stallion blood.

All this took place so long ago
that it seems very late
for you still to ba saking, What happened?
But you do,
and one answer may be
once a dog ran into you
out of instinct, madness, or unignorable orders.
The meaning of blood and dent
you cannot beat from fender
Is not clear, except that it is
clearly not related to guilt,
as you were on you way to attempting the right
thing, and there is no dog left
on hyphenated lines to be run down again
and again, becoming tread for tires, nightmares.

No one can tell you if what
by now maybe limps with pain
or lies in a swoon of guts
chose you out of so many travelers,
a wild thing bent on collision, wreckage,
ancient memory trace
in which a mound of dry bones
must precede each resurrection.

No one can tell you how this will turn out
or if what darts in and out
deserves your serious attention.

Perhaps it is only the first
in a long list of encounters,
perparation for mastering the skill
of trusting yourself again to steering
or sleep with the scantest information,
of leaving more than you ever dreamed
unfinished, up in air, becoming
what it becomes.

At the Wharf, Yorktown: For All Tracks Made in San

Because this is a July night,
more sunbathers have vanished
than in January, leaving only tracks
like clues traffic-jamming the whole length of beach.

If I were a better liar
I would swear I have come
searching the feet of true direction,
lost while ambling north by south,
sideways by transister radio,
snatched straight up into sky.

But this beach is no abstraction.
On a real night in October
I walked here, in love again
with love
who wore a green leisure suit
who wore eyes like the ocean
who wore a mouth that told me,

over lobster dinner, how this
was what he'd waited for all of his life.
(Yes, this is what we wait for
all of our lives.)
Afterwards, we dug for augers,
drill-shells that bore into sand
as soon as they're dumped by the ocean,
each packed with one microscopic blot
of poison, barely enough
to put an amoeba to sleep.
Nor are the augers abstractions:
we filled our pockets, took them home,
strung them into necklaces as proof.

How many real days in April
found me here, in love again
with love
who wore cut-offs
who wore eyes that bounced my face
off his prescription lenses,
who wore a mouth that told me,
over cheese-and-cracker lunch,
how he had never known anything like this.
(Each time we have never known
anything like this.)
Afterwards we scooped augers
into our jeans; back home I filled a Mason jar
(augers are useless as ashtrays)
with evidence.

Some parts of these stories
are lies. Fossilized, what will our tracks
prove to archaeologists? Tonight
is a real night in July
and I am here alone
in love again
with love
who wears air
shifting across a million mismatched
shoes. When I address you, Love,
stand in one place until I'm finished—
Who gave you permission to bear
all your faces
into the heart of swept dunes?

Love, I think I am coming to know you
through your infinite directions, your series
of practice drills, perfecting each march
into the heart by training on sand:
no wonder we never hear you come in.

This is what we wait for
all of our lives. Each time
we have never known anything like it.
This digging for augers,
this turn and return,

these cupped palms aching to be filled.   **63**

Carnegie-Mellon Poetry

1975
The Living and the Dead, Ann Hayes
In the Face of Descent, T. Alan Broughton

1976
The Week the Dirigible Came, Jay Meek
Full of Lust and Good Usage, Stephen Dunn

1977
*How I Escaped from the Labyrinth and
    Other Poems*, Philip Dacey
The Lady from the Dark Green Hills, Jim Hall
For Luck: Poems 1962-1977, H.L. Van Brunt
By the Wreckmaster's Cottage, Paula Rankin

1978
New & Selected Poems, James Bertolino
The Sun Fetcher, Michael Dennis Browne
A Circus of Needs, Stephen Dunn
The Crowd Inside, Elizabeth Libbey

1979
Paying Back the Sea, Philip Dow
Swimmer in the Rain, Robert Wallace
Far From Home, T. Alan Broughton
The Room Where Summer Ends, Peter Cooley
No Ordinary World, Mekeel McBride

1980
*And the Man Who Was Traveling Never Got
    Home*, H.L. Van Brunt
Drawing on the Walls, Jay Meek
The Yellow House on the Corner, Rita Dove
The 8-Step Grapevine, Dara Wier
The Mating Reflex, Jim Hall

1981
A Little Faith, John Skoyles
Augers, Paula Rankin
Walking Home from the Icehouse, Vern Rutsala